The Internationally Recognized

Speaker from Ghana,

AJ AJ

by Ben Gothard,

Founder & CEO of Gothard Enterprises LLC

Author of CEO at 20: A Little Book for Big Dreams

ISBN-10: 1946941026

ISBN-13: 978-1946941022

Project EGG

ENTREPRENEURS GATHERING FOR GROWTH

Project EGG is an elite network of entrepreneurs, authors & incredible people who problem solve, bounce ideas off of each other, share their stories and succeed together.

This mastermind includes people from around the world who are making a difference right now. We have a truly incredible group of people, like CEOs, CFOs, founders, national best-selling authors, inventors, marketers, coaches, consultants, musicians, speakers, and many many more entrepreneurs from every corner of the globe.

In the official Project EGG podcast, hosted by myself, Ben Gothard, different members of the group are interviewed. Each interview is a deep-dive into the life of the guest as both the guest and I drill down into entrepreneurship and personal development. By sharing their life and experiences, we can all learn something valuable.

This book is a transcription of the interview, unedited. Hopefully you can get as much out of the interview as I did hosting it!

Ben: Welcome to Project EGG. Today, we're here with AJ AJ from the U.K. How are you doing this morning?

AJ: I'm doing phenomenal. How are you doing yourself?

Ben: Good, good. Thank you. Alright, let's jump into it. The first question I have for you today is: what is your story?

AJ: My story is I'm originally from Ghana; born and bred in Ghana in West Africa. I lived in Italy for the past seven years with family and went to school and try to fit myself within their Italian environment. By about 2010, I moved to the United Kingdom to fit in education and have much more opportunity to build up my life and my career. So being here in the U.K., I discovered a way where I could tap myself into personal development. It was there where a gentleman approached me in 2013, and he said I got something for you and I said, why not let's have a look?

So I started in a network marketing environment where the personal development growth was massive and productive which touched my life. I was still at the time looking for what I have to do with my life and what is the calling. Being in that platform and having the opportunity laid out, I understood the concept and I got that. I have something redeemed that I could step out for my comfort zone and give back to the people; give back to the world's people who need to understand the concept of purpose and living the life that they deserve.

That's where the journey started from and we've been on a journey helping people set up a platform, kind of similar to my platform called AOA which stands for Arise Organize Aspire and we go out with motivational speakers, mentors, one-on-one to help young children, young people or even adults know still don't know their purpose of life and what they live for. The journey is big and the story is massive. We just want to reach out to people.

Ben: That's great. You said you were approached by somebody and I think that mentors are always a huge part of anybody's success story. Could you point to any mentors that you've had in your life that had provided inspiration or motivation?

AJ: Mentors I've had have been indirect mentors in the form of that I don't connect to them personally, but I would say some of them I've met face to face by being in the network marketing environment. I will say I met great people, great leaders which they've helped me directly and indirectly. I would probably say one of my greatest mentors I've looked up to is Eric Worry and people like Lest Brown. I go see a lot of speakers like Eric Thompson; a lot of great mentors that I learned from. Great people. I think that I've had a lot of mentors and that I've been learning from on a day-to-day basis.

Ben: So you're talking about how you were breaking in to the personal development scene; what do you actively do today to help people develop themselves and reach a higher level of performance, happiness, or personal growth?

AJ: Well what I do today is I tap into all the great things and good things that I've learned and instilled within me personally. I give back to the people by guiding them from scratch — it depends on who I'm talking to and what's their level of personal development and growth they have; what makes you tap into where I could see they would need help. I just give back basically what I've learned in the past few years, and also what I'm still learning and pass on the energy back to the people. Give them that sort of positive view of what they could get from what I've learned so far.

Ben: Right. You're saying that learning is really important. Just for everybody else who may not know good places to turn to for personal development—for where they could go to for more information or for a better place to learn—where would you point those people? Where would you start them on the journey?

AJ: I think to start on the journey, you have to just go get some books, do some research, speak to people who are already successful, people who have already been there—if you want to fly, you fly with eagles; if you want to be a pigeon, you stay with pigeons all day long. The person you want to become, you got to find those people; you got to look for those people and those people are the first step that you have to take first, and then you will get all the materials that you need to personally develop yourself. For example, you can go online, find out how to develop yourself—read some books and some great inspirational books that could help you mindset wise. You could find all of them online. I believe we live in a generation where people trust online or computer technology services, so I think that's the greatest place you could tap into. YouTube is great—a lot of videos there that you could start learning to develop your mind on a day-to-day basis.

Ben: And of course they could always come to you for some help for personal development, right?

AJ: Sure, you can come to me. You can tap into my Facebook, AJ AJ. Online, you can add me on Instagram, Augustine O Aygei; the same name for my Twitter. Also I got a Facebook page which is the same name as well, Augustine O

Aygei which you can tap into. I am also available by email at talk@augustineoaygei.com.

Ben: Awesome. In your story earlier, you were saying how you've been moving from place to place but for personal and professional reasons. Do you think that all the different places that you've been have influenced your personal development and have shaped your life in any significant way?

AJ: Well yes, sure. I believe that people go to places for reasons and it could be the bad but it could be the good reason. Sometimes, it could be like what you're looking for might not accomplish and you just have to move on. I think that being in a different environment has developed me to become the person that I am today even though I'm still a work in progress, learning and adding more, because you can't stop learning. I think that they've impacted good stuff—positive and negative things in my life but I look more to the positive things. You get the opportunity to learn from different people, meet different types of people from different backgrounds, different professionalism, different culture, and different things which get you to understand how life is. I think it's really helped.

Ben: Absolutely. You said you're in the U.K. now. Do you plan on staying there for a while or is there a big move coming in the future?

AJ: I'm the person who likes to travel. I like to spread my wings and go places because I believe if you want something, once you've learned something, you don't need to stay in one place; you have to go around the world and share as much as you can. So I like to travel. I wouldn't say U.K. is my last stop but I think in the future, there are great things to be had and I'm looking forward to greatness. I'm thinking of going around in a couple of months ahead. I'm a man of adventure and I just like to tap into different places.

Ben: Moving forward, you said you had a lot of big goals, you want to fly with eagles—and I think it's a brilliant quote by the way. What do you think is the one most important thing that you want to accomplish in your lifetime?

AJ: The one most important thing that I want to accomplish in my lifetime is to have more time. Have more time to do a lot of things that most people couldn't do, such as going around and help inspire others. Make sure the fulfillment you give back to the people. Go around and do what I love best which is spending time with positive vibes and trying to rebuild broken walls and people and the things that other people need. One of the greatest goals for me is to have a lot of time to spend with family in the future — quality time, I mean. Live the life and memories and moments where people can look up to you and say, because of your service, dedication, and because of this person, through God's help, we are no longer what we are. So that's one of the great goals and to be able to tap and live like a sign that will last forever to eternity.

Ben: Kind of like a legacy, right? I'm always a big proponent of passing on advice to others and trying to help out—it seems like you are too, so what is the one biggest piece of advice that you could give to other people who are trying to follow in your footsteps?

AJ: What I give to other people who are trying to follow in my footsteps is that patience is key in whatever you do. You have to have that patience with whatever you're doing in this life. If you don't have patience and you're looking for something that could give you speed or instant result, it's not going to happen overnight. It's not going to happen just like that because as we know, great things take time. You have to have that key to wait in good days and enjoy the process and enjoy the journey. Work hard and smart alongside it because one thing I always say is that your future is right and is good only if you work hard for it. One thing I will say to people who are trying to work towards the same path that I've chosen to work on is to be patient because that's the only key that most people lack nowadays. Patience is key, and with God, all things are possible.

Ben: Okay, so I just have one more question for you. Is there anything about you that you would like to share that I didn't ask you about?

AJ: Well, anything about me that I would like to share is that I'm a man full of ambition and action. I know, for example, is that the vision is really big and one thing I want people to understand is that life isn't easy, but it's easy only when you follow the principles of life and when you pay attention to it. I hear a lot of people all the time everywhere saying, I want to be successful, I want to be that, I want to be that...but they are not ready to pay the price for it. Until you're ready to pay the price for it, you won't get anything. So people need to be ready when they say certain things and when they mean that they want to be successful for real, because life itself isn't easy. You have to enjoy the process while you're on the journey, because that's what will get you to the end. As we say, the dream is free but the journey is sold separately. So that's the only thing I'd probably add to it.

Ben: Right, that's a great quote. Before I let you go, I know that you just competed in a contest recently. You want to tell everybody about that?

AJ: Great, yeah. I got nominated for the REEBA Awards 2016—REEBA Awards is made for entrepreneurs and I got selected as an influential entrepreneur for 2016 which I'm grateful for. I just want to thank people who voted and helped us reach out to the people.

*****Since the filming of this interview, AJ AJ actually won that award!!*****

Ben: Absolutely. Alright AJ, well thank you very much for coming to the interview today. Best of luck to you moving forward.

AJ: Thank you Mr. Ben and thank you for your time as well. I appreciate it.